NEW YORK

The Empire State

BY
JOHN HAMILTON

Abdo & Daughters

An imprint of Abdo Publishing | abdopublishing.com

abdopublishing.com

Published by ABDO Publishing, a division of ABDO, PO Box 398166, Minneapolis, Minnesota 55439. Copyright © 2017 by Abdo Consulting Group, Inc. International copyrights reserved in all countries. No part of this book may be reproduced in any form without written permission from the publisher. ABDO & Daughters™ is a trademark and logo of ABDO Publishing.

Printed in the United States of America, North Mankato, Minnesota.
052016
092016

THIS BOOK CONTAINS RECYCLED MATERIALS

Editor: Sue Hamilton   **Contributing Editor:** Bridget O'Brien
Graphic Design: Sue Hamilton
Cover Art Direction: Candice Keimig   **Cover Photo Selection:** Neil Klinepier
Cover Photo: iStock
Interior Images: Alamy, AP, Brooklyn Nets, Buffalo Bills, Buffalo Sabres, Comstock, Daniel Tripp, Delaware Art Museum, Dreamstime, General Motors, Getty, Granger, History in Full Color-Restoration/Colorization, Great Western Catskills Tourism Office, International Olympic Committee, iStock, John Hamilton, Library of Congress, Mile High Maps, Nancy Bishop, New Netherland Institute, New York City Football Club, New York Giants, New York Islanders, New York Jets, New York Knicks, New York Liberty, New York Mets, New York Public Library, New York Rangers, New York Red Bulls, New York Yankees, North Wind, One Mile Up, State of New York Pure Maple Syrup, The Athenaeum/Robert Walter Weir, & Wikimedia.

Statistics: *State and City Populations*, U.S. Census Bureau, July 1, 2015/2014 estimates; *Land and Water Area*, U.S. Census Bureau, 2010 Census, MAF/TIGER database; *State Temperature Extremes*, NOAA National Climatic Data Center; *Climatology and Average Annual Precipitation*, NOAA National Climatic Data Center, 1980-2015 statewide averages; *State Highest and Lowest Points*, NOAA National Geodetic Survey.

Websites: To learn more about the United States, visit booklinks.abdopublishing.com. These links are routinely monitored and updated to provide the most current information available.

Cataloging-in-Publication Data

Names: Hamilton, John, 1959- author.
Title: New York / by John Hamilton.
Description: Minneapolis, MN : Abdo Publishing, [2017] | Series: The United
    States of America | Includes index.
Identifiers: LCCN 2015957624 | ISBN 9781680783346 (lib. bdg.) |
    ISBN 9781680774382 (ebook)
Subjects: LCSH: New York--Juvenile literature.
Classification: DDC 974.7--dc23
LC record available at http://lccn.loc.gov/2015957624

CONTENTS

THE EMPIRE STATE

New York is one of the most populous and powerful states in the nation. Its vast wealth and natural resources prompted George Washington in 1785 to write that New York was "the seat of the empire."

The Empire State is like two states wrapped into one. To the north are quiet country lanes, farmers' markets, mountains, and roaring waterfalls.

The south is dominated by New York City. Nicknamed "The Big Apple," it is the biggest metropolis in the country. The city is filled with more than 8 million people—about 2 of every 5 people in the state. It is a center for banking, transportation, publishing, theater, and so much more. It is a diverse city that never sleeps, where the pace of life is so fast it spawned the phrase "in a New York minute." Home to skyscrapers, the United Nations, and the Statue of Liberty, New York City is a symbol of freedom and opportunity for millions of immigrants who come to America.

The beautiful Adirondack Mountains are a popular destination in northern New York state.

The Statue of Liberty stands in New York Harbor.

QUICK FACTS

Name: New York was named in honor of James, the Duke of York and Albany, who later became King James II of England.

State Capital: Albany, population 98,566

Date of Statehood: July 26, 1788 (11th state)

Population: 19,795,791 (4th-most populous state)

Area (Total Land and Water): 54,555 square miles (141,297 sq km), 27th-largest state

Largest City: New York City, population 8,491,079

Nickname: The Empire State

Motto: *Excelsior* (Ever Upward)

State Bird: Bluebird

State Flower: Rose

State Gemstone: Garnet

State Tree: Sugar Maple

State Song: "I Love New York"

Highest Point: Mount Marcy, 5,344 feet (1,629 m)

Mount Marcy

Lowest Point: Atlantic Ocean, 0 feet (0 m)

Average July High Temperature: 79°F (26°C)

Atlantic Ocean

Record High Temperature: 108°F (42°C), in Troy on July 22, 1926

Average January Low Temperature: 12°F (-11°C)

Martin Van Buren

Record Low Temperature: -52°F (-47°C), in Old Forge on February 18, 1979

Average Annual Precipitation: 43 inches (109 cm)

Millard Fillmore

Number of U.S. Senators: 2

Number of U.S. Representatives: 27

Theodore Roosevelt

U.S. Presidents Born in NY:
Martin Van Buren (1782-1862),
Millard Fillmore (1800-1874),
Theodore Roosevelt (1858-1919),
Franklin Roosevelt (1882-1945)

Franklin Roosevelt

U.S. Postal Service Abbreviation: NY

GEOGRAPHY

New York is in the Mid-Atlantic region of the United States. The biggest geographic region within New York is the Appalachian Upland. Sometimes called the Allegheny Plateau, it covers about a third of New York, including most of the western and central parts of the state. The Appalachian Upland includes the Catskill Mountains and the Finger Lakes areas. They are prized for outdoor recreation such as skiing, hiking, and boating.

The Atlantic Coastal Plain is a low-lying, flat region along the Atlantic Ocean coast. It includes Long Island and Staten Island. It has good farmland that produces potatoes, plus other vegetables and fruits.

The Adirondack Mountains are part of the Adirondack Upland, in the northeastern part of New York. These ancient peaks are filled with forests, lakes, streams, wildlife, and hiking paths. Mount Marcy is New York's highest point. It rises 5,344 feet (1,629 m) above sea level.

The Catskill Mountains are part of the Appalachian Upland. The beautiful area is enjoyed by hikers and other outdoor lovers.

New York's total land and water area is 54,555 square miles (141,297 sq km). It is the 27th-largest state. The state capital is Albany.

The Hudson Highlands include steep mountains on both sides of the Hudson River as it flows through southeastern New York. The southern part of this region includes the island of Manhattan. It is called the Manhattan Prong. Nestled between the two areas is a small flat area called the Newark Lowlands.

The remainder of the Hudson River Valley and all of the Mohawk River Valley is within the Hudson-Mohawk Lowlands. The Hudson and Mohawk Rivers were very important transportation routes early in New York's history. This low-lying area has good soil for farming crops such as potatoes and apples. The state capital of Albany is in this region. Just to the east of the Hudson-Mohawk Lowlands are the Taconic Mountains.

Niagara Falls

New York borders two Great Lakes on its western side: Lake Erie and Lake Ontario. The Erie-Ontario Lowlands and St. Lawrence-Champlain Lowlands are rolling hills that follow the shoreline and extend northward toward New York's northern border with Quebec, Canada. The Niagara River connects Lake Erie and Lake Ontario. It includes spectacular Niagara Falls.

Besides Lake Erie and Lake Ontario, New York has more than 7,600 lakes and ponds. Some of the larger lakes include Lake Champlain, Lake George, and Oneida Lake. Long Island Sound is another large body of water. Part of the Atlantic Ocean, it rests between the north shore of Long Island and the state of Connecticut.

New York also contains more than 70,000 miles (112,654 km) of rivers and streams. Besides the Hudson and Mohawk Rivers, other important waterways include the Allegheny, Delaware, Genesee, and Susquehanna Rivers.

GEOGRAPHY

CLIMATE AND
WEATHER

Even though New York's southern tip touches the Atlantic Ocean, overall the state has a humid continental climate. The weather often changes, and there are great differences between the northern part of the state and the south. There are four seasons, with warm, humid summers and cold winters.

Warm, humid air from the south often collides with cooler and drier wind from the north. This usually brings cool, humid conditions. Cloudy days are common. Near the coast, the summers are hotter, but the winters are milder. The Adirondack and Catskill Mountains have very cold winters and much snow.

New York normally sees a statewide average July high temperature of 79°F (26°C). The record high temperature was 108°F (42°C), in the city of Troy, on July 22, 1926. In winter, the average January low temperature is 12°F (-11°C). The record low occurred on February 18, 1979, in Old Forge. On that day, the thermometer plunged to -52°F (-47°C).

Western New York experiences lake-effect snow. Cool, dry air mixes with warm lake water, resulting in huge amounts of snow.

New York gets plenty of rain and snow, averaging 43 inches (109 cm) of precipitation yearly. Tornadoes are rare. Hurricanes sometimes damage low-lying areas, including Long Island, which juts into the Atlantic Ocean.

In 2011, Hurricane Irene flooded low-lying parts of coastal New York, including an area under the Brooklyn Bridge.

PLANTS AND
ANIMALS

Forests cover about 63 percent of New York. That is nearly 18.9 million acres (7.6 million ha) of land. The majority of the state's forests are privately owned. However, New York owns large amounts of forestland. It manages more than 787,000 acres (318,488 ha) that are set aside as state forests.

Adirondack Park is the largest state park in the United States. Enclosing most of the heavily forested Adirondack Mountains, the park includes both public and private lands. There are heavy restrictions on development and logging, both to preserve the area's natural beauty and to protect vital water supplies.

There are nearly 150 kinds of trees in New York. Most are deciduous hardwoods that turn color and lose their leaves in the autumn. Many birds and animals make their homes in these woodlands. There are also many pine trees in the Adirondack Mountains.

Common trees found in New York include ash, aspen, beech, birch, chestnut, cherry, dogwood, elm, hickory, pine, poplar, walnut, and willow. The official state tree is the sugar maple.

Sugar maples, New York's official state tree, line a path in Windsor, New York.

New York's forests and meadows are filled with many kinds of shrubs, bushes, and wildflowers. They include daisies, black-eyed Susans, goldenrod, cardinal flowers, flowering raspberry, and wild blackberries. The official state bush is the lilac, and the state flower is the rose.

Common wild animals found throughout New York include white-tailed deer, bobcats, coyotes, porcupines, foxes, fishers, minks, moose, muskrats, otters, raccoons, skunks, and weasels. Black bears are most often found in the Adirondack and Catskill Mountains.

The official state animal is the beaver. The large rodents were highly prized by trappers starting in the 1600s. The beaver pelt trade was one of the reasons Dutch and English settlers first came to the New York area.

North American Beaver

Hundreds of species of birds can be seen winging their way across the skies of New York. The state is along the major Atlantic Flyway migration route. Common birds include ring-necked pheasants, ruffed grouse, wild turkeys, Canadian geese, wood ducks, canvasback ducks, mallards, great horned owls, bald eagles, red-tailed hawks, great blue herons, terns, gulls, cardinals, doves, blue jays, American robins, and black-capped chickadees.

The eastern bluebird is the official state bird of New York. Males are colored bright blue. The songbirds prefer grasslands and scattered forestland. Many New Yorkers build bluebird nesting boxes and place them on fence posts.

A baby bluebird on a nesting box demands food.

New York's inland freshwater lakes and streams teem with fish. They include bass, catfish, herring, perch, pike, salmon, sturgeon, and sunfish.

Brook trout is the official state fish. Saltwater fish off the Atlantic Ocean coast include striped bass, flounder, and scup.

17

HISTORY

The first people to live in New York came to the area about 10,000 years ago. These Paleo-Indians were the ancestors of today's Native Americans. They hunted large animals, such as mastodons, with stone spear points.

By the time the first European explorers arrived in the 1500s, two powerful groups of Native Americans had settled the land. They were the Iroquois and Algonquian cultures. The Algonquian-speaking people (which included the Mohican and Munsee tribes) lived near the Atlantic Ocean coast. The Iroquois people (including the Mohawk, Oneida, Cayuga, Onondaga, and Seneca tribes) lived in the lands to the west.

Before Europeans arrived in the 1500s, Manhattan Island Native Americans lived in long houses made of bound-together tree saplings, topped with bark.

Native Americans view Henry Hudson's landing in New York Harbor in 1609.

Giovanni da Verrazzano

The first European to visit New York was Italian explorer Giovanni da Verrazzano, who was working for King Francis I of France. Verrazzano sailed into New York Bay in 1524. In 1609, English explorer Henry Hudson sailed up the Hudson River. He was working for the Dutch. They claimed the territory as a colony and named it New Netherland.

In 1624, Dutch settlers built the first permanent European settlement in the New York area. It was called Fort Orange, near today's Albany. They traded for furs with the local Native Americans.

Dutch official Peter Minuit offers trade goods to Native Americans in exchange for the island of Manhattan on May 24, 1626.

In 1625, the Dutch constructed a fort and settlement on the southern tip of Manhattan Island. The following year, they bought the island from a group of Native Americans. They called their settlement New Amsterdam. Years later, it would become New York City.

In 1664, England took control of New Netherland during a war with the Dutch. Three English warships forced the Dutch to surrender at New Amsterdam. The English renamed the city and region New York, after James, the Duke of York and Albany, who would later become King James II. New York was briefly recaptured by the Dutch in 1673, but it was soon returned to the English after both sides signed a peace treaty.

In 1776, New York joined the other 12 American colonies in their struggle for independence from Great Britain. New York was the site of many battles during the Revolutionary War (1775-1783). In August 1776, General George Washington's army barely escaped destruction at the Battle of Long Island. British forces captured New York City and occupied it for the rest of the war. But during the 1777 Battle of Saratoga, in east-central New York, the Patriots won a hard-fought victory. It was a major turning point in the war.

After a string of Patriot battlefield victories, a peace treaty with Great Britain was signed in 1783. British forces finally left New York City. On July 26, 1788, New York ratified, or approved, the United States Constitution, becoming the 11th state to join the Union. New York City became a banking center for the young nation.

On August 27, 1776, the Continental Army fought the Battle of Long Island against overwhelming British forces. Two days later, General George Washington had no choice but to retreat with his troops, leaving New York City to the British.

The Erie Canal allowed people and goods to be transported from New York to the Great Lakes.

In the early 1800s, settlers pushed into western New York and other territories beyond. Better transportation was needed to carry passengers and heavy goods. After eight years of construction, the Erie Canal was opened in 1825. The waterway linked Lake Erie with the Hudson River. Barges pulled by horses carried factory goods, farm products, and immigrants traveling westward to America's heartland. Cities near the Great Lakes, such as Buffalo and Rochester, grew and prospered.

Before the Civil War (1861-1865), New York was strongly against slavery. When war broke out, it sent 360,000 soldiers to fight for the Union against the Southern Confederacy, more than any other Northern state.

After the Civil War, New York's economy boomed. Millions of immigrants entered the United States through the Ellis Island inspection station, greeted by the inspiring sight of the nearby Statue of Liberty. New factories, skyscrapers, and shops sprang up. New York became a financial powerhouse.

The Great Depression started on Wall Street when the stock market crashed in 1929. Millions of people lost their jobs and businesses. The economy improved during World War II (1939-1945). New York City's harbor was a busy shipping center for the military.

In the last half of the 20th century and into the 2000s, New York has faced many challenges, including the terrorist attacks of September 11, 2001. The Empire State always bounces back. Today, it continues its role as one of the most important places in the nation.

The Tribute in Light honors the people who died in the Twin Towers of the World Trade Center. The two columns of light glow each year on September 11.

DID YOU KNOW?

The Statue of Liberty under construction in Paris in 1884.

Immigrants view the Statue of Liberty from New York's Ellis Island in 1930.

• The Statue of Liberty was unveiled on October 28, 1886. A gift from the people of France, the colossus stands on Liberty Island in New York Harbor, in New York City. For decades it was an inspiring sight for millions of immigrants who came to America by boat. From the foundation to the tip of its torch, the statue is 305 feet (93 m) tall. Its total weight is 225 tons (204 metric tons). Designed by French sculptor Frédéric Auguste Bartholdi, the statue represents the Roman goddess Libertas, a symbol of freedom.

• Lake-effect snow is a kind of weather event that often happens in western New York. When winter weather systems drift across the Great Lakes, they pick up evaporated water. When the clouds blow over land, they dump massive amounts of snow. The western New York cities of Syracuse, Rochester, Buffalo, and Binghamton are among the snowiest cities in the country. In February 2016, a single storm system dropped more than 3 feet (.9 m) of snow on some areas of western New York.

• The horrific terrorist attacks of September 11, 2001, killed almost 3,000 people and destroyed the Twin Towers of New York City's World Trade Center. Nearly 12 years after the attacks, a new building has risen in the skyline of Manhattan. One World Trade Center soars 1,776 feet (541 m) tall. It is the tallest building in the western hemisphere. About 48,000 tons (43,545 metric tons) of structural steel were used in its construction, the equivalent of 22,500 automobiles.

DID YOU KNOW?

PEOPLE

Franklin D. Roosevelt (1882-1945) was the 32nd president of the United States. He was elected four times, the most of any president. He served as a Democrat from 1933 to 1945, when he died in office. Before his time as president, he served as the governor of New York, from 1929 to 1932. Roosevelt guided the country through the most troubled times in its history. His plan to help the country's economy recover from the Great Depression was called the New Deal. He also led the United States through most of World War II. Roosevelt was born in Hyde Park, New York.

Theodore Roosevelt (1858-1919) was the 26th president of the United States. A Republican, he served from 1901 to 1909. He also served as governor of New York from 1899 to 1900, and as assistant secretary of the Navy from 1897 to 1898. In 1898, he led the United States Cavalry's Rough Riders in Cuba during the Spanish-American War. As president, Roosevelt supported laws to punish dishonest companies. He also led the fight to conserve America's wilderness lands. He helped get the Panama Canal built, and expanded the United States Navy. In 1906, he won the Nobel Peace Prize for helping end a war between Russia and Japan. Roosevelt was born in New York City.

Jennifer Lopez (1969-) is an actress, singer, and producer. Also known as J. Lo, she is one of the most successful Hispanic performers in the world. She began her career in the late 1980s, starring in Hollywood films such as *Selena* and *The Wedding Planner*. In 1999, she released her debut album, *On the 6*. She went on to sell more than 60 million records worldwide. Lopez was born in the Bronx, New York.

Fiorello La Guardia (1882-1947) was the mayor of New York City from 1934 to 1945. He served three terms. His leadership helped the city recover from the Great Depression of the 1930s. A Republican reformer, he supported women's rights, fought political corruption, and expanded housing for the poor. New York City's LaGuardia Airport is named after the popular mayor. La Guardia was born in the Greenwich Village neighborhood of New York City.

Jay Z (1969-) is a rapper and businessman. Many people consider him to be one of the most successful and influential hip-hop artists of all time. He has sold more than 100 million records worldwide. He has won 21 Grammy Awards for his music. His most successful albums include *Reasonable Doubt*, *The Blueprint*, and *The Black Album*. He married singer Beyoncé in 2008. Jay Z was born in Brooklyn, New York.

Lou Gehrig (1903-1941) was a first baseman for the New York Yankees for 17 seasons. He played from 1923 to 1939. A great hitter and extremely durable, he was nicknamed "The Iron Horse." He was twice named the American League's Most Valuable Player. His life was cut short when he contracted ALS, the disease commonly called Lou Gehrig's disease today. He was inducted into the Baseball Hall of Fame in 1939. Lou Gehrig was born and grew up in Manhattan, New York.

CITIES

Albany is the capital of New York. Its population is 98,566. It is located along the west bank of the Hudson River, in east-central New York. First settled in 1614, it is one of the oldest cities in America. It has been New York's capital since 1797. Today, it is a center of commerce, manufacturing, and the arts. State government, education, and health care are major employers. Many technology companies have recently moved to the city. There are several universities, including the State University of New York at Albany, which enrolls more than 17,500 students. The city's annual Tulip Festival celebrates Dutch heritage.

New York City is by far the largest city in the United States. Its population is 8,491,079. Together with its surrounding communities, the metropolitan area is home to more than 20 million people. New York City contains five boroughs, which are like small cities, or counties, merged into one. The boroughs include Manhattan, the Bronx, Queens, Brooklyn, and Staten Island. Each borough has many distinct neighborhoods, such as Manhattan's Financial District (including Wall Street), or Brooklyn's Coney Island beachfront. New York City is one of the most densely populated cities in the world. It is a leader in trade, finance, education, theater, fashion, publishing, architecture, and much more. Many immigrants pass through or settle in New York City. More than 800 languages are spoken in the city.

Buffalo is located in far-western New York, along the shores of Lake Erie. It is at the head of the Niagara River, just south of Niagara Falls. Buffalo is the state's second-largest city. Its population is 258,703. It has long been a transportation center, ever since the Erie Canal opened in 1825. Manufacturing and trade boomed in the 1800s. Today, Buffalo relies more on financial services, higher education, and technology companies. It is home to many theaters, art galleries, and orchestras. Buffalo is famous for its many ethnic restaurants and fine cuisine, especially Buffalo chicken wings.

Rochester is in western New York, near the southern shore of Lake Ontario. It is New York's third-largest city. Its population is 209,983. In the 1800s, waterpower from the Genesee River helped the city's factories produce goods such as flour and clothing. Today, Rochester is home to many technology companies, including Eastman Kodak. The University of Rochester includes the acclaimed Eastman School of Music.

Syracuse is New York's fifth-largest city. Its population is 144,263. It is located in central New York, in the Finger Lakes region. It is a center for trade, transportation, and manufacturing. The city is home to Syracuse University, which enrolls more than 21,000 students. Syracuse also hosts the Great New York State Fair, which attracts almost one million visitors each year.

TRANSPORTATION

New York became a powerful state early in its history because of its major transportation routes, including the Hudson River and the Erie Canal. In the later part of the 1800s, railroads and roads added to the state's transportation system.

Today, there are 114,728 miles (184,637 km) of public roadways in New York. Busy Interstates I-90, I-86, and I-88 run mostly east and west across the state. Interstates I-81 and I-87 travel north and south.

New York City has a vast commuter network. It includes a subway system that carries more than 1.7 billion passengers yearly.

The Port of New York and New Jersey is the busiest port on the East Coast. It handles millions of tons of cargo worth more than $200 billion annually.

Manhattan's Grand Central Terminal is one of the busiest train stations in the world. It has 44 train platforms and serves almost 200,000 people a day.

A BNSF locomotive hauls tank cars through Upstate New York.

New York has 39 freight railroads operating on 3,447 miles (5,547 km) of track. The most common bulk products hauled include chemicals, coal, food and farm products, stone, and scrap items.

There are 15 main commercial airports in New York. The two largest serve the New York City area. John F. Kennedy International Airport handles more than 53 million passengers yearly. LaGuardia Airport handles 27 million passengers.

John F. Kennedy International Airport is located in Queens, New York City.

NATURAL RESOURCES

There are approximately 35,500 farms in New York. They cover 7.2 million acres (2.9 million ha) of land, which is about 21 percent of the state's total land area. Agriculture adds about $5.4 billion to New York's economy each year.

New York ranks third in the nation for producing milk from cows. The state's most valuable crops include corn, soybeans, hay, cabbage, beans, potatoes, onions, wheat, squash, cucumbers, strawberries, oats, pumpkins, cherries, and apples. There are many vineyards in the Finger Lakes and Hudson River Valley areas. The state is the nation's second-largest producer of maple syrup, making more than 600,000 gallons (2.3 million l) annually.

Sap is collected from maple trees to make maple syrup in Alexander, New York.

Commercial fishing vessels line the docks at Montauk Harbor in New York.

About 63 percent of New York's land area is forested. The forest industry employs more than 60,000 people and adds $4.6 billion to the state economy.

New York's largest commercial fishing port is in Montauk, which is on the eastern tip of Long Island. Catches include bluefish, black sea bass, flounder, oysters, and clams.

Mining adds $1.5 billion yearly to New York's economy. Sand and gravel are dug in 90 percent of the state's mines. Other products include garnet, salt, talc, and zinc.

NATURAL RESOURCES

INDUSTRY

New York's economy is huge. It rivals those of entire countries in the world! Its gross state product—the value of all its goods and services—was $1.44 trillion in 2015.

New York factories produce computers and other electronics, paper and printing products, scientific instruments, photographic equipment, and apparel.

Like many other states, New York today relies greatly on the service industry. Instead of manufacturing products, service companies sell services to businesses and consumers. They include businesses such as advertising, financial services, health care, insurance, restaurants, retail stores, law, marketing, and tourism.

GM **Tonawanda** Powertrain

TONAWANDA ENGINE PLANT

EXIT

ENTRANCE

Auto engines are produced at the General Motors plant in Tonawanda, New York.

New York City is the powerhouse of the state's economy. Manhattan's Financial District, including Wall Street, is a center for banking and finance. Trillions of dollars in business transactions are handled at the New York Stock Exchange.

The New York Stock Exchange (large flag) began in 1817. It stands today at 11 Wall Street in Lower Manhattan.

Many publishing and broadcasting giants are located in New York City. They include the *New York Times*, the *Wall Street Journal*, ABC, CBS, NBC, FOX, and Univision. There are also dozens of book and magazine publishers, radio stations, and music labels in the city.

With its many landmarks, shops, and resorts, New York is a popular place to visit. Tourists add about $60 billion each year to New York's economy.

SPORTS

New York is home to dozens of professional sports teams. The Buffalo Bills, the New York Giants, and the New York Jets all play in the National Football League (NFL). The Giants and Jets play their home games in nearby East Rutherford, New Jersey. The Giants have won the Super Bowl four times, while the Jets have won once.

The New York Yankees and the New York Mets are Major League Baseball (MLB) teams. The Yankees have won the World Series 27 times, while the Mets have won twice.

There are three National Hockey League (NHL) teams in the state. They include the New York Islanders, the New York Rangers, and the Buffalo Sabres. The Islanders and Rangers each have won the Stanley Cup championship trophy four times.

New York's National Basketball Association (NBA) teams include the New York Knicks and the Brooklyn Nets. The Knicks have won the NBA Finals championship twice.

The New York Liberty plays in the Women's National Basketball Association (WNBA). New York City FC is the state's Major League Soccer (MLS) team. The New York Red Bulls represent the state, but play in New Jersey.

Winter sports are big in New York, especially at ski resorts in the Catskill and Adirondack Mountains. Lake Placid hosted the Olympic Winter Games in 1932 and 1980.

Skiers get ready to head down Plattekill Mountain near Roxbury, New York.

ENTERTAINMENT

New York is famous for its arts and culture. Many of the world's best painters, architects, musicians, writers, and photographers make their home in New York City.

Some of the most acclaimed art museums in New York include the Guggenheim Museum, the Metropolitan Museum of Art, the Museum of Modern Art, and the Whitney Museum of American Art.

Broadway is the heart of Manhattan's Theater District. It is home to dozens of theaters, restaurants, and hotels. At night, the district, especially world-famous Times Square, is lit by a dazzling array of lights and billboards, which is how it got its nickname, "The Great White Way."

Times Square

Radio City Music Hall is one of the world's largest indoor theaters, with about 6,000 seats. Since 1932, more than 300 million people have attended one of its shows.

Besides theaters, New York is filled with symphony orchestras, bands, ballet troupes, fashion shows, and much more. Major landmarks include the Statue of Liberty, the Empire State Building, the National September 11 Memorial & Museum, the American Museum of Natural History, the Brooklyn Bridge, Radio City Music Hall, Ellis Island, and much more.

Popular zoos are located in Central Park and the Bronx. There are also zoos in Buffalo and Rochester. Coney Island, in Brooklyn, is a popular resort and amusement park area, and is also home to the New York Aquarium. There are also countless festivals and fairs held throughout New York.

TIMELINE

8000 BC—Paleo-Indians first come to the New York area.

1500s—Iroquois- and Algonquian-speaking Native Americans settle into villages.

1524—Explorer Giovanni da Verrazzano is the first European to see present-day New York.

1609—Explorer Henry Hudson sails up the Hudson River and claims the New York area for the Dutch. The Dutch call the new territory New Netherland.

1624—Dutch settlers build Fort Orange, the first permanent European settlement in New Netherland.

1625—Dutch settlers build a fort on the southern tip of Manhattan Island. It eventually becomes New York City.

1664—British forces take control of the Dutch colony and rename it New York.

1754–1763—The French and Indian War takes place. Important battles occur at Lake George and Lake Champlain in New York.

1776—George Washington and his American troops narrowly escape destruction at the Battle of Long Island. British forces occupy New York City.

1777—American forces win a major victory at the Battle of Saratoga during the Revolutionary War.

1788—New York becomes the 11ᵗʰ state in the Union.

1825—The Erie Canal is completed.

1861—The Civil War begins. New York stays in the Union, sending hundreds of thousands of troops to fight the Southern Confederacy.

1892—Ellis Island becomes the main entry facility for immigrants. More than 12 million immigrants are processed at Ellis Island between 1892 and 1954.

1931—The Empire State Building is completed. It remains the tallest building in the world until the World Trade Center towers are completed in 1970.

2001—Terrorists attack New York City's World Trade Center on September 11.

2012—Hurricane Sandy destroys many homes and businesses along New York's Atlantic Ocean coastal region.

2014—One World Trade Center opens. The new skyscraper is the tallest building in the Western Hemisphere.

GLOSSARY

ALS or Lou Gehrig's Disease

Amyotrophic lateral sclerosis is a progressively worsening disease that affects the muscles and spinal cord of a sufferer. Communication from the brain to the muscles is disrupted, resulting in muscles becoming weaker and weaker, until the sufferer's body can no longer survive. The disease is also known as Lou Gehrig's disease, named after the famous New York Yankees baseball player who suffered and died from ALS.

Canal

A waterway that carries freight and people in boats. Canals often connect lakes and rivers.

Colony

A group of people who settle in a distant territory but remain citizens of their native country.

Immigrants

People who make a foreign country their home. Many immigrants to the United States in the 1800s settled in New York, or passed through on their way to other states.

Lake-Effect Snow

A winter weather system that causes unusually large amounts of snow to fall. The weather systems pick up moisture when they blow over large bodies of water, such as Lake Erie, and then dump snow on land areas close to the shore.

Long Island Sound

A body of water that is part of the Atlantic Ocean. It is between Connecticut and the north shore of New York's Long Island. It is a drowned valley carved out by glaciers thousands of years ago. When the glaciers melted, the sea level rose and covered the valley. Long Island Sound is nearly 110 miles (177 km) long and 21 miles (34 km) at its widest.

Revolutionary War

The war fought between the American colonies and Great Britain from 1775-1783. It is also known as the American Revolution, or the War of Independence.

Rough Riders

A nickname given to the United States Army's 1st United States Volunteer Cavalry. When led by Theodore Roosevelt in 1898, it became one of the most famous American military fighting units in history.

Spanish-American War

A war started in April 1898 between Spain and the United States. The war was fought to help the islands of Puerto Rico, Cuba, and the Philippeans gain freedom from Spain. The war ended in December 1898 with Spain giving up the islands by signing the Treaty of Paris.

Territory

An area of land controlled by a country's government. Early in its history, the United States held much territory in lands west of the established states. People settled these lands and formed communities. Eventually, the territories became states.

INDEX